MASTERING ART

CARTOONS

Anthony Hodge

STARGAZER BOOKS

CONTENTS

© Aladdin Books Ltd 2005

New edition published in the United States in 2005 by:
Stargazer Books
c/o The Creative Company
123 South Broad Street
P.O. Box 227
Mankato, Minnesota 56002

Designer: Phil Kay
Editors: Jen Green,
       Harriet Brown
Drawings: Anthony Hodge
Illustrations:
Ron Hayward Associates

Printed in UAE
All rights reserved

Library of Congress Cataloging-in-Publication Data

Hodge, Anthony.
   [Cartooning]
   Cartoons / Anthony Hodge.-- New ed.
     p. cm. -- (Mastering art)
   Includes index.
   ISBN 1-932799-02-8 (alk. paper)
     1. Cartooning--Technique--Juvenile literature. I. Title.

NC1320.H527 2004
741.5--dc22
                          2004040175

Introduction

Cartooning is about having fun and developing a new skill at the same time. If you are the sort of person who sees the funny side of things, this is the chance to get some of your ideas down on paper. And if you've always wanted to have adventures, now you can invent strip cartoons in which anything can happen.

This book introduces you to different kinds of cartoons and to the wide range of materials you can use for cartooning. You don't need to be great at drawing; many cartoons are based on a few simple lines.

The first cartoons

Originally, a cartoon was a sketch made in preparation for a more finished work. Today, a cartoon is a particular kind of drawing, direct and effective, often funny. The best cartoons usually say something about life that people are often too afraid to talk about.

▶ "These four cartoons are of characters who just emerged when I started doodling. There's no limit to the number and variety of types waiting to jump out of your head, too. The one at the top right thinks he is drawing something very funny-I hope this happens to you!"

Jokes and Caricatures

Over the next pages you will discover the different types of cartoon and the materials they can be drawn with.

Visual jokes

The simplest cartoon of all is a picture that makes a joke. The drawing itself can be funny, or can surprise us. Alternatively, it's the cartoon character who's about to get a surprise; we can see it coming but the character can't!

Some cartoon jokes don't need words; others rely on words to communicate their meaning.

Pencil and felt-tip marker

The most basic tools for cartooning are pencils and felt-tip markers. A soft pencil produces a friendly line (below left). You can go over a sketch in pencil with felt-tip marker or ink, and then erase any mistakes.

A fine felt-tip marker makes an elegant line (below middle). A thick marker (below right) produces bold, solid marks.

Many kinds of paper are suitable for cartooning. Thin paper is useful for tracing and redrawing images if you make a mistake.

Caricature

A caricature is a drawing of a real person in which individual features, like the size of the person's nose or the shape of the chin, are exaggerated. Yet, somehow a likeness is achieved. In fact, if done cleverly, a caricature can look more like the individual than he or she does in real life!

For thousands of years, cartoonists have been making caricatures of public figures. Depending on the artist, they can be kind or cruel, flattering or grotesque.

Ink, charcoal and conté

Pen and ink, charcoal, and conté are all lively materials suitable for caricaturing. Ink can be used with a dip-pen or a fountain pen, and with nibs of different sizes. Ink makes free, expressive lines (below left).

Charcoal produces a dark line for dramatic portraits (below middle). It can produce a rough and ready look, or can be smudged to make shadows.

Conté comes in shades of brown or gray. It produces soft, warm marks good for caricatures like the hairy, bear-like person below right.

Cartoon Strips and Animation

Cartoon strips

Cartoon strips are a sequence of individual cartoons that tell a story. The principle is to show how actions develop through a series of images. Take a look at the range of styles that can be used.

We often enjoy cartoon strips without noticing the techniques that artists use to show close-up or long distance views, to indicate drama, tension, or a change of pace. Filmmakers and animators use similar techniques to produce the same kinds of effects.

Cartooning in color

You can create pale and dark tones by pressing lightly or heavily, and new colors by laying one color over another. Watercolor and gouache (below middle) are both good for cartooning. Watercolor is washed on thinly and is transparent. Gouache is denser and opaque. For both, you will need to use thick paper.

Chunky felt-tip markers (below right) cover the paper quickly and evenly; thin ones are good for outlines.

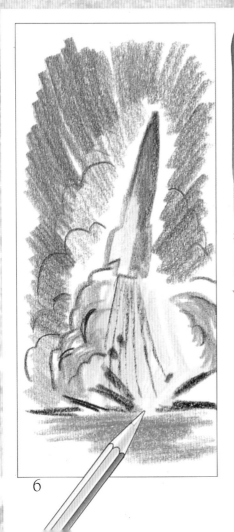  

Animation

Animation is a way of bringing pictures to life. When we watch a modern cartoon movie, we seem to see a smooth sequence of movement. It's hard to believe we are actually looking at thousands of single pictures, each one slightly different than the last. They change in front of our eyes so quickly we can't see when one image replaces another.

Later, we will look at the various techniques animators use. You can practice some of these tricks yourself.

Painting on acetate

For the purposes of animation, cartoons are painted on sheets of clear plastic called acetate. Both sides of the acetate are used, as shown below. The image is drawn on one side with a special oil-based pen called an o.h.p. (overhead projector) pen. The image is colored in on the other side using gouache or acrylic paint. Computers are often used in animation because they can reproduce a picture quickly and accurately.

Basics: Heads Galore

All cartooning styles rely on a few basic ideas. Let's look at cartooning heads. Faces are everywhere if you know how to look—in trees, clouds, even in a coat hanging on the door. For the cartoonist, imagination is very important.

Eggheads

A cartoon head usually starts life as an egg shape. The basic ingredients of a face are two dots for eyes, an L-shape for a nose, and a line for the mouth. The way you combine these features can create all kinds of characters (see the faces below left).

Begin your cartooning career by experimenting with the basic features. Then try using different shapes, choosing a particular shape for the head and echoing the same shape as you draw in the features.

Positioning the features

Eyes set far apart look confident; eyes set close together (bottom right) look shy. Features placed at the bottom of the head look clever; features placed at the top appear self-satisfied.

Shapes and personalities

The shape of the head suggests personality. A pear-shaped face looks sad, a square head looks mechanical. A curvy face looks flabby and a star-shape is full of energy.

▶ "Once you start drawing, ideas will come. I didn't plan the character shown right, but added details as I went along, as though I were creating an actress for a role."

Faces step-by-step

Try building your own cartoon personalities. Start with a head shape and add features, hair, and clothes. Draw your character again, now with a different expression.

▼ "Expressions affect all the facial features, especially the mouth. Practice some expressions yourself in front of a mirror. Cartoon expressions are even more pronounced."

Basics: Getting Things Moving

Action cartoons need to be presented simply and clearly. The secret of drawing figures on the move is to start with a few lines and build on them from there.

Stick figures

The skeleton is the basis of all figures. The stick figure represents the skeleton. Try a series of stick figures before you begin a more developed drawing.

▶ "Action can be summarized in one line. To get your imagination going, sketch a line at random and see what it can be turned into! To emphasize movement, add speed lines and details like the flying pipe and hat."

▼ "Fill the pages of your sketchbook with stick people running and jumping. When you're happy with your action people, start to flesh them out into sausage figures, as shown below."

Basics: Points of View

"Everybody's got to be somewhere," as Spike Milligan said. Where are you right now? Everyone reading this will give a different answer. In cartoons, the action can be set anywhere. The best jokes often have more to do with the setting than what the characters are doing or saying.

How things change size

Cartoon backgrounds are usually kept simple. In cartoons, things that are close-up are drawn bigger than those farther away. This is called perspective. Look at the girl on the railroad track (below bottom left). The train is of course bigger than she is, but it appears smaller because it's farther away.

Looking up and down

Perspective affects how things appear from different angles, as you can see from the cartoons on the right. The knight looks very different from various angles: straight on, from below, and above. Parts of his body loom large, or dwindle away, depending on how close they are to us. It takes practice to get this right, and it helps to work with stick men.

▶ "Different angles increase the drama and impact of your cartooning. The face-on view is the least dramatic. Seen from below, looking up, the knight's feet and fists look huge. Viewed from above, his helmet and sword seem to zoom toward us as he sweeps past."

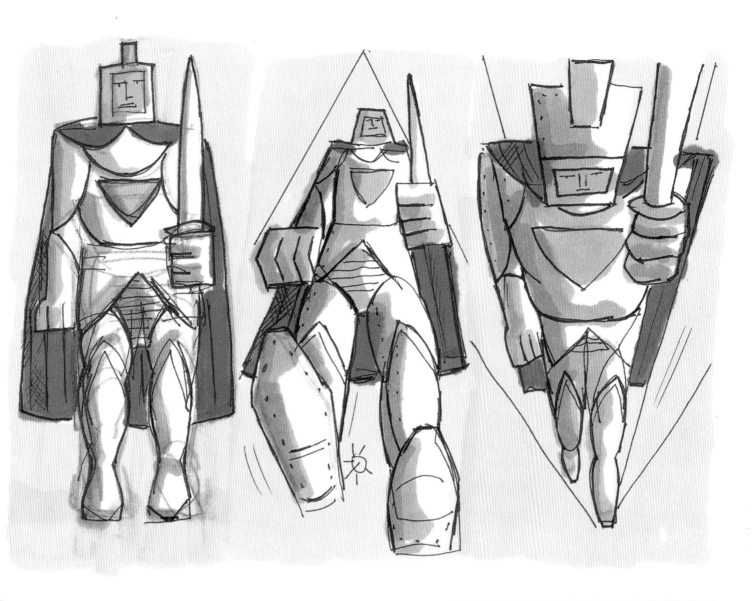

Tiny or tremendous?

Background can completely alter how we understand a cartoon. The top two cartoons on the left show how the same girl seems to change size, depending on the background. Practice putting your own character in different settings.

Putting things in perspective

The girl on the railroad track is an example of a kind of perspective called linear or line perspective.

The lines of the railroad track run parallel, but they appear to meet at a point on the horizon called vanishing point. All parallel lines follow this rule. Sketching lines in pencil that meet at a vanishing point can help place things in perspective.

Perspective can also be achieved by overlapping. The girl, bottom right, overlaps and conceals some of the houses, indicating that she is standing in front of them. The car overlaps the pavement and appears closest to us.

Cartoon Puns

At its simplest, a cartoon is something that makes us laugh. On this page we will look at the most basic jokes of all, those without words or captions, and explore how you can think of some of your own.

Visual puns

Many jokes without words rely on visual puns. A visual pun is a joke based on a shape with two meanings, just as a verbal pun is based on a word with two meanings. The cartoon at the top of the opposite page is an example of a visual pun.

Doodle power

Develop your ability to find visual puns by doodling. Draw a simple shape, like the rectangle, coil, and zigzag patterns shown in red below. Have a good look at the lines. What do they suggest to you? Turn the paper around and look at it from each side. Your squiggle could turn into anything—it's a matter of letting your imagination run riot.

Generating ideas

A good way of coming up with ideas is to doodle. The shapes below might help to generate ideas. For example, you could merge the clown and the skier—how strange, a man skiing down a clown's hat!

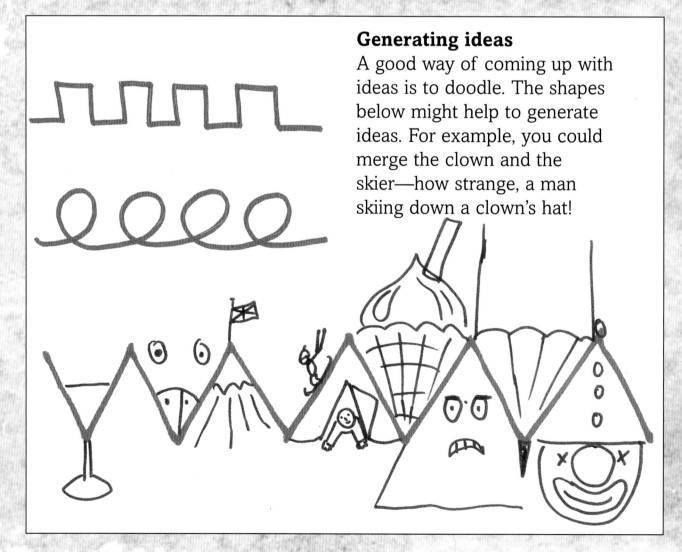

Doing two jobs

You can also make jokes about objects with two functions. The blindfold appears in both pictures below, but in the second, it is put to an unexpected use. Let your imagination loose on other objects that can have more than one use, such as umbrellas, baby carriages, and walking sticks.

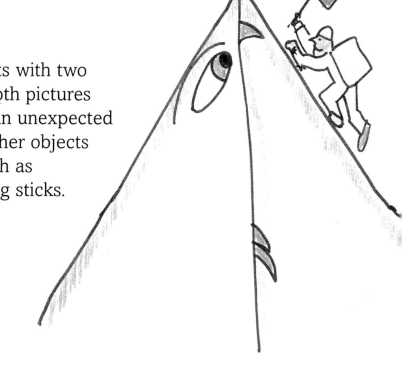

▶ "This visual pun is drawn from the sketch on the previous page. The humor in many cartoons is based on anticipation: something is about to happen, but the character involved is not aware of it-yet!"

Getting your point across

The joke here is about the blindfold. It's colored black to make it obvious. All the details in the first picture—the guns, the charcters' expressions—lead us to expect the worst. In the second picture, the details reappear but are changed, emphasizing the contrast in mood.

Words Can Help You

The punch line game

In cartoon jokes, the meaning is often conveyed in the caption (words) below the picture, known as the punch line. The project here is to think of as many ways as possible to illustrate a simple punch line such as,

"I suppose you find that funny." Other punch lines you could try include, "Don't look now but...," "I thought you said there were no side-effects," or even, "We can't go on meeting like this." Sketch rough ideas and try to develop one or two farther.

Do you read me?

In cartoon speech, words themselves are only part of the message. The shape you write in and the lettering you use can help to convey the message.

Speech usually appears within a round bubble, but a speech box with straight lines can suggest angry words. Thought clouds can tell you what a character is thinking.

Pow!

Loud noise is expressed in large colored letters. The style of lettering and the shape in which the word appears increase the effect. A star-shape implies an impact or explosion. Make sure your words are legible.

Shipwrecked? Stranded?

Below are the two most common dilemmas that cartoon characters find themselves in. Practice the punch line game in reverse, by thinking of as many punch lines as possible for these two images. Consider different interpretations of the pictures.

Lost in the jungle or all at sea?

Cartoonists often return to classic comic situations such as hospitals, prisons, or car accidents. Why are these situations funny? They are often dangerous, embarrassing, or unexpected situations that we wouldn't like to be in ourselves!

The joke is often about how ordinary people react to extraordinary situations. Someone carried away by a monster might, for example, worry about whether they locked the front door. Funny things happen in everyday life, too. Note down ideas—they might help you come up with a punch line or a cartoon in the future.

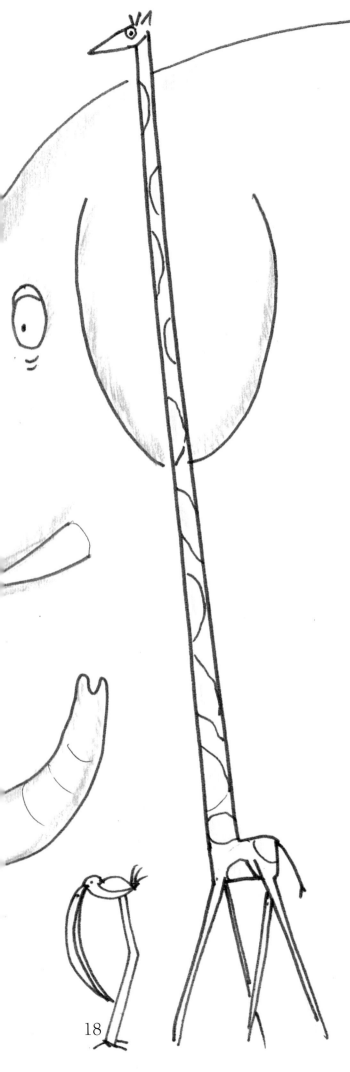

Caricature

Have you got a nickname? If you haven't, someone you know probably has. Nicknames are like shorthand; we use them to sum people up, not always kindly. If they stick, it's usually because they pinpoint something about that person's appearance or personality.

Caricatures are visual nicknames. They focus on certain characteristics and emphasize them. Like most cartoons, they simplify and exaggerate what we see.

Animal crackers

Some caricaturists say that it helps them to think of a person as an animal. When we draw animals from imagination, we focus on their most obvious features and emphasize them. Try caricaturing animals yourself, either from imagination or from photographs. Do a realistic drawing first and then exaggerate it into a caricature.

◄ "The main thing about an elephant is size. To emphasize this, I've made mine so big it can't fit on the page, but I've left enough clues to identify it. The first thing you notice about a giraffe is the long neck. Wading birds have long legs and curved beaks, so these are the things I've chosen to exaggerate."

Stretching a point

The same idea applies to caricaturing both people and animals. You will need to get to know the face of your victim well. Study the face and decide which features are most important. Make these stand out even more.

Not just heads

What you emphasize is up to you. Two cartoonists will produce very different caricatures of the same person. Caricatures can be about bodies, too. The size of the stomach, the length of the arms, and the posture, can all add to your caricature.

What's in a face?

In caricature try to sum up and exaggerate. The first caricature has focused on the boy's hair and grin; the second (top right) has made the most of the glasses, pointed nose, and glum mouth. The girl gets messier hair, a pug nose, and a more fixed expression, and the man (bottom right) has an even snootier look.

Do-It-Yourself Caricature

Now you know how caricature works, it's time to try some of your own. First, choose your subject. Pick someone you know well, or a famous person you admire, or even one whom you dislike!

That's typical!
You will need to consider what pose and what habits are most typical of your subject. Capturing the essence of someone's personality need not involve drawing their face or even much of their body. If Grandpa spends most of his time in an armchair reading the newspaper, you could draw the newspaper with two hands holding it and just the top of his head surrounded by the chair. Add smoke from a pipe and his red slippers to make it obvious who it is.

The right tool for the job
Make sure the drawing materials you choose match your subject. Pencils, pen and ink, charcoal, and conté all have a very different "feel." Charcoal (below left) has a rich, soft look. Pen and ink has a spontaneous quality. The caricature below right uses an ink wash to create shadows and a seedy look.

Clothes always help to identify your subject. Some people's clothes or style are so individual that a back view may be enough. Some people like to hide behind their accessories—look at the charcoal portrait far left on the opposite page.

▼ "Caricatures of famous people can be fun: I chose John Wayne (below). First, I did a drawing from a photograph to familiarize myself with my subject. I noted a square chin, and the lift of one eyebrow. From movies I remembered his habit of talking out of one side of his mouth. As John Wayne is best known for cowboy parts, I added a hat, kerchief, and checked shirt."

21

Creating a Superhero

A cartoon strip is a series of pictures that tell a story. The next two pages demonstrate how to create your own cartoon strip. The first step is to invent your own characters.

What do superheroes have in common? Most superheroes are based on a combination of certain characteristics. Identifying these will help you build your own characters.

Factor X

Some superheroes come from other planets but most are from Earth; they are ordinary creatures who have acquired a special ability, often as a result of some extraordinary event. They might get their powers from radiation or from something very ordinary. A superhero has his or her own territory, a particular location to patrol. Cities are popular, and so is, of course, outer space.

Missions and superskills

All superheroes have a cause—to fight villains or to right a particular injustice in the world. Your superhero needs a mission, and a special ability. Think about the superpower you would most like to have yourself!

A superpower can be extra strength, sight, or hearing. Or it can be X-ray vision, or the ability to change shape. A superhero associated with an animal takes on the creature's powers—so the owl girl above might be able to see in the dark.

Developing a script

You can develop your superhero by thinking about costume, weaknesses, likes and dislikes, sidekicks, and friends. Sometimes it is best just to start an adventure and see how your superhero performs!

What makes a good storyline?

Cartoon scripts usually begin with a problem: a crime or mystery that is often the work of a villain. It may be almost too late but the hero learns of the trouble and steps in.

Meanwhile, problems may mount up; friends may be captured or hurt. At the last moment, the hero arrives on the scene and saves the day. There is often a celebration before the hero heads home.

▶ "My superhero, Cartoonman, is a cool customer. Here he is studying his script, unconcerned by the battle raging around him. To find out what problems lie in store for him, see the script, above right."

CARTOONMAN'S FIRST ADVENTURE
Rocketwoman is guiding her spaceship across the galaxy when the engine develops a fault. Forced to crash land on an unknown planet, she is besieged by alien life forms. Using his superhearing, Cartoonman learns of the danger. He speeds to the planet and takes control of the situation. Returning Rocketwoman to her own planet, he receives a hero's send-off and returns to base.

Your Own Cartoon Strip

Once you've invented your superhero and developed a script, it's time to plan how to illustrate the action. In the best cartoon strips, the reader follows the plot, and also enjoys the strip as a visual adventure. Varying the size and shape of your pictures or *frames*, or changing the scale and perspective, all add to the impact of your cartoon.

A story in a single page

Sketch out some rough designs or *layouts* for your story. Only illustrate the main points, and leave the rest for the reader to imagine. Different frame sizes will be appropriate for showing key moments of action and for conveying necessary information.

Color is important. Characters and locations should each appear a certain color so that the reader can easily recognize them. Use strong colors for foregrounds, and quieter colors for backgrounds.

Once you're happy with your layout, fill in your frames.

▶ "Cartoonman's first adventure is illustrated on the opposite page. I've used speech bubbles to include some more tips on page layout. Try to replace my tips with an actual script."

Laying out your page

Below are three sample page layouts. Try to see your page of cartoons as a single picture, made up of different elements. Using a limited number of colors will help this.

As these examples illustrate, cartoon frames don't have to be rectangular. Some images will fit better into a different shape. A diagonal line leads the eye to the next frame; ovals and circles liven up the page.

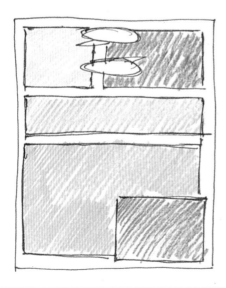  

Flick Book Animation

Making moving pictures is called animation. The most simple form of animation is the flick book.

All you need is a pencil and a long strip of paper about three inches wide. The paper should be thin enough to see through, but shouldn't be too fragile. Fold the strip in half, crease it, and open it out again.

Before and after

Think of an action or event you want to illustrate, involving "before" and "after" positions. Draw the first stage of your idea on the second page of the two-page "book." In the example below, this is the man with smooth hair. Fold the first page of the book back over the image. You should be able to make out some of the picture underneath.

For your flick book to be effective, some parts of your image should remain the same. Trace these through the paper, then draw in the different parts that will appear to move.

Trial run

Once you've drawn the second picture, roll it up tightly around a pencil. Hold the paper down, as shown below. Then move your pencil left and right, to reveal your "before" and "after" pictures alternately.

Sample flick books

Below are two "before" and "after" ideas. In the first, the man kicks the ball in the air, and in the second, two people fall in love.

Animated notebooks

Now try a further sequence of action. You'll need a notebook with blank pages of thin paper. Think of an action, and decide how many stages you need to illustrate it.

Draw the key stages in your notebook first, shown here as pages 1, 5, and 9. Start with the last in your sequence and trace the unmoving parts of the picture through the paper. Then fill in the pictures in between, working from back to front.

▶ "Once all your stages are complete, flick the pages of your notebook and watch your picture come to life! The more accurate your tracing is, the more effective this will be."

Moving Pictures

If you had the power to slow life down, you might see movement as a series of tiny changes. The project here is about seeing complex action in this way. It will help to develop the skill of seeing as an animator does—in slow motion, one step at a time.

In your mind's eye

Think of an action sequence like the one below. As before, you will need to concentrate on the key moments of action. These are your *key frames*, the beginning and end of the movement, and two or three other stages in between.

Once you're happy with your key frames, you'll need to sketch in the action in between. These stages are known as "in-betweeners." You can use tracing paper to reproduce the parts of your drawing that remain the same, and even the parts that look the same but have moved position.

Key frames and in-betweeners

Artists working on full-length cartoon films use the system of key frames and in-betweeners. The artist does the key frames and computers fill in the action sequence—the in-between frames.

▼ "Not so easy for you and me, perhaps, but anything is possible in the world of animation. The four key frames are shown in color, and the in-betweeners are inserted to complete the sequence."

Using a light box

Animators often draw on acetate (see page 7). To trace the parts of the image that remain the same in the next frame, you can use a light box (below).

The completed acetate sheet is pinned in position. A second sheet is laid on top. Once the light box is switched on, the first image can be seen clearly, and parts of it traced.

Animation

Have you any idea how many separate pictures are needed for a full length cartoon film? Thousands? In fact, it's nearly a million. This work used to be done by hand. Today, much of it can be done by computers.

Once a cartoon image is finished, it is photographed individually, and becomes one frame of the film. There are 24 of these frames in one second of film time. When the film is shown in a movie theater, the frames change so fast that we see nonstop action.

▼ "You can use a light box to see the outlines of your cartoon more clearly."

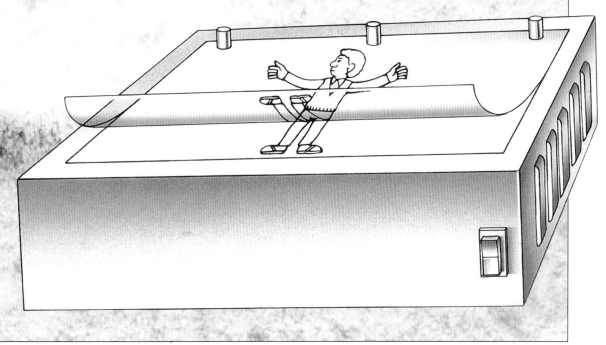

Cartoon Projects

Some of the techniques in this book can be used to make gifts for your family and friends.

Your own comic

Aim high by publishing your own comic book. Include all your best jokes, and the exploits of your cartoon strip heroes. Invent adventures with plots to be continued in the next issue; your friends will soon be clamoring for the next edition. Why not combine efforts with a friend? You could try doing alternate pictures, making it up as you go along.

Cartoon cards

Many of your drawings will make great greetings cards. Your best two-frame joke, with the first picture on the front and the punch line inside, will work well.

Caricature cards are another possibility, but be careful who you send them to! On the left, you can see someone receiving a caricature birthday card with mixed feelings.

Your favorite flick books can also make excellent cards. You could even include a pencil and instructions. The front page of your flick book must be on thin paper, or it won't roll around the pencil. For the other cards you could choose to work on thicker paper or cardboard.

Practical Tips

Protecting your equipment
Keeping your drawing equipment safe is important. Store your paper, pencils, and drawing pads together in one place. Protect your paper by storing it away in a drawer.

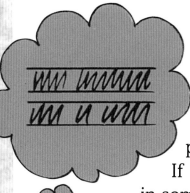

Getting rid of mistakes
Everyone makes mistakes. Erasers take care of pencil errors.

If your drawing is in something like felt-tip marker, tracing is a good way of saving the parts you're happy with.

You can cover mistakes with opaque white watercolor that you can buy from an art store.

You could also cut a fresh piece of paper to cover your mistake and paste it over the top with glue.

Working with felt-tip markers
Felt-tip markers are excellent color tools. Use them to fill in areas of paper quickly and evenly. Remember that felt-tip markers

soak through thin paper, so don't have anything precious underneath.

Stick to light colors, and use strong ones for detail. Allow time for one color to dry before applying another next to it, otherwise your work might smudge.

Fixative
If you're working with charcoal or conté, you will need to seal your work with fixative to stop it smudging. This is available from art stores. Place your finished drawing in a well-ventilated area and spray fixative evenly over it. Be careful not to get any in your eyes.

The dictionary game
Coming up with ideas for cartoons, particularly for cartoon jokes, is easier for some of us than others. One exercise that can encourage the flow of ideas is the dictionary game. Get a dictionary and pick two words from it at random. Think up a way of linking them in a picture. If nothing springs to mind, try another word, but don't cheat too much!

Index